iii

LETS GO !

PUBLISH

Govt. Must Stop Ripping Off Seniors' Social Security!

Hey Buddy, Seniors Can No Longer Spare a Dime?

The most beleaguered citizens in the United States are our senior citizens. Seniors are victims of government. It should not be so; but it is easy to explain. There is not one senior citizen member of Congress, who actually depends on Social Security to make ends meet. How is it then that they get to cast their magic wands annually to determine the cost of living increase due Seniors.

Congressional inflation estimates unfortunately are nothing close to the reality of the real price increases Seniors actually pay every-day at supermarkets and clothing stores in America? The law on SSR has been distorted and Seniors need and deserve a massive adjustment. It is up to Seniors to make sure Congress knows that it has not delivered. Perhaps when Seniors are responsible for sending members home for good after the next election, the Congress will understand.

If President Obama had another heart, some say it would be lonesome. For eight years, Seniors served as the former President's personal punching bag as he stubbornly refused to give Seniors a break. Obama even tried to reduce senior benefits with his chained CPI proposal. Then, he took more than $700 Billion from Medicare to fund his signature legislation known as Obamacare. Democrats, the ones who claim Republicans have no hearts are all Tin Men on the SSR issue and their main man for eight years, Barack H. Obama had no regard at all for Seniors. He claimed otherwise but worked to reduce SSR benefits for the duration of his eight years in office.

Wimpy RINO Republicans without the courage of Donald Trump, permitted the former President to decrease the livelihood of Seniors and chose not to fire back at the former president with the gumption they now show when opposing Trump. They chose to do nothing to help Seniors. Mike Huckabee was the first Republican to complain when he publicly accused "illegals, prostitutes, pimps, (and) drug dealers" of freeloading off the Social Security system during the first GOP primary debate way back on August. 6, 2015. This freeloading must be paid back to Seniors. Despite President Trump's problems with Republican RINOs, Seniors pray he still has the energy to help.

During his campaign, candidate Trump promised to protect Social Security without cutting benefits. I wrote this book to help remind the President that a huge SSR monthly increase is the right medicine and it must be done ASAP before more Seniors suffer. Seniors, if denied the proper increase, need more than just accepting the bad medicine of the past. They need to be paid back for the abuses to the system over the years that Mike Huckabee and others have cited. If you don't have a mom or a dad who are hurting because their Social Security "check" does not even pay for their meals, you can't know how bad it is in America for "poor" Seniors.

What should President Trump do in the absence of any Congressional leadership? His positive actions would include paying back Medicare from Obamacare. It would include increasing SSR benefits over the next four years of the Trump term by at least 15% per year. Even this will not make up for what was stolen from Seniors using a fraudulent cost of living percentage. President Trump knows that revenue flows from elimination of waste, fraud, & abuse and he can direct that American oil reserves can provide ample cash for strategic emergency make-up funding for senior benefits. For Seniors, he can also use the cash from solving the illegal resident crisis by cracking down on illegal welfare by fake IDs using an innovative resident visa plan. What would you pay to see every senior in America smile because buying a fresh loaf of bread and a dozen eggs is no longer a big issue in their lives? Seniors ask for nothing more than to be made whole for the intentional fraud in Congress's CPI calculations and to use an accurate measurement of the cost of living and the out-of-pocket expenses endured by Seniors.

My concern is that the good President Trump, as the sitting president, may be so insulated from the reality he knew as a candidate, might sit idle and permit an unfair inflation rate put more and more Seniors in the poorhouse. He must make up for all the past bad CPIs at once. American can take care of her Seniors if we so desire. In this book, we tell you how things can and must be made lots better for penniless Seniors, whose scant increases get wiped out all the time by Medicare increases. You'll be surprised as to how much sense it makes. President Trump cannot let Seniors down.

BRIAN W. KELLY

Copyright © 2018 Brian W. Kelly   Editor Brian P. Kelly
                                         Author Brian W. Kelly
Title: **Stop Ripping Off Seniors' SSR to Boost the US Treasury!**
Subtitle: Hey Buddy, Seniors Can No Longer Spare a Dime?

Referenced Material: *The information in this book has been obtained through personal and third party observations, interviews, and copious research. Where unique information has been provided or extracted from other sources, those sources are acknowledged within the text of the book itself or at the end of the chapter in the Sources Section. Thus, there are no formal footnotes nor is there a bibliography section. Any picture that does not have a source was taken from various sites on the Internet with no credit attached. If resource owners would like credit in the next printing, please email publisher.*

Published by: LETS GO PUBLISH!
Publisher: Brian P. Kelly
Editor: Brian P. Kelly
Cover Design: Brian W. Kelly
Mail Location: P.O. Box 621, Wilkes-Barre, PA 18703
Web site   www.letsgopublish.com

Library of Congress Copyright Information Pending

ISBN Information: The International Standard Book Number (ISBN) is a unique machine-readable identification number, which marks any book unmistakably. The ISBN is the clear standard in the book industry. 159 countries and territories are officially ISBN members.

978-1-947402-64-5

The price for this work is :   **$6.95 USD**

10   9   8   7   6   5   4   3   2   1

Release Date: October 2019

Dedication

I dedicate this book
To the Kelly Twins, my sister and brother, Mary Daniels
and Joseph Kelly, and their wonderful families

They are the youngest members of the Irene and Edward J.
Kelly family.

Mary Alice and her husband Bill Daniels are blessed with
three Children and seven grandchildren. Megan and Jason
Kauwell, and their son Nathan and daughter Charlotte;
Elizabeth and Brian Ginochetti, and their daughters Sophia
and Elise, and their son Luke; Billy Daniels, and his son
Jaxen Cole and daughter Skylar

Joseph Aloysius and Diane Kelly are blessed with two
daughters and three grandchildren. Tara and Christopher
Bryk, their son Aiden, and their daughter Zoey; Colleen
Kelly and her daughter Caitlin Marie.

Thank you all for your help and smiles and the best!

Acknowledgments

I would like to thank many, many people for helping me in this effort.

I appreciate all the help that I have received in putting this book together as well as all of my other 180 published books.

My printed acknowledgments had become so large that book readers "complained" about going through too many pages to get to page one of the text.

And, so to permit me more flexibility, I put my acknowledgment list online, and it continues to grow. Believe it or not, it once cost about a dollar more to print each book.

Thank you and God bless you all for your help. In particular thanks are given to Wily Ky Eueley.

Please check out www.letsgopublish.com to read the latest version of my heartfelt acknowledgments as updated for this book. Click the bottom of the Main menu!

To sum up my acknowledgments, as I do in every book that I have written, I am compelled to offer that I am truly convinced that "the only thing you can do alone in life is fail." Thanks to my family, good friends, and a wonderful helping team, I was never alone.

Table of Contents

Preface:

Congress & the President must act now to avoid a crisis!

Somebody will say that the US cannot afford to pay for Seniors to be OK! I say that we cannot afford not to do what is right, This is America.

If somebody says we cannot afford to assure that Seniors can lead lives in which the poorhouse is not a constant threat, please tell them to read Chapter 4 from start to finish and use their imagination. We can afford making Seniors whole again and we must. The dirtiest politicians in America colluded so they would not have to take the real cost of living into consideration for the last thirty years or so. Nobody in America wants this perpetration to stand, especially Seniors who are about to lose their homes and who are scraping to find a good meal.

For eight years of President Obama's regime, it was not very safe to be a senior citizen. It is still not safe, but many Seniors are hopeful with Donald Trump in charge, that things will change. In former president Obama's heart, he had to know that this batch of Seniors did not trust him very much to do the right thing by them. Seniors got exactly what they expected from Obama – nothing.

Only low information Seniors, and there are far too many for the good of the US senior citizen population, continued to the end to give the former president the benefit of the doubt. I guess this was because they listened to the corrupt fake-news mainstream media- CNN, MSNBC, ABC, & CBS --and they read the biased v Seniors New York Times. All Seniors and the rest of America have to wake up. Every family has Seniors who depend on SSR benefits. We must all end the cheating perpetrated by a corrupt Congress. Our power comes from our vote.

Even today, too many starving Seniors do not fault the former president, though they would if they really knew what he did to them. Worse than that, if they knew how bad he tried to make it, but failed, Seniors would be enraged. You'll learn what that was in this book. President Obama did his best to destroy the lives of senior citizens.

It is a documented fact that the most beleaguered citizens in the United States today are senior citizens. Some are so respectful of authority that they become dumb when a Democrat suggests they have it made because of all great Democratic programs. Try living on that.

For eight years, any senior paying attention noticed that they were serving as former President Obama's personal punching bags. He knew that in their hearts, many, who knew what he was up to had little regard for him.

They had him pegged right as a man who would take away their last drop of water if he could. They were right. There is lots more inside this book to help Seniors move to action to assure that SSR increases are fair and that the government brings Seniors back to where they should be—after all the government lying on the inflation rate.

Yes, I am talking about large annual increases in COLA for the next four to eight years to help Seniors get back most of what they lost because of all the fraud associated with the government's cost of living adjustments.

You are going to love this book as it tells it like it is. Feel free to contact your Congressman and President Trump so that they know how you feel. One day we will all be Seniors.

I wish you all the best

Brian P. Kelly, Publisher
P.O Box 621 Wilkes-Barre, Pennsylvania 18703

About the Author

Brian W. Kelly is a retired Assistant Professor in the Business Information Technology (BIT) program at Marywood University, where he also served as the IBM i and midrange systems technical advisor to the IT faculty. Kelly developed and taught many college and professional courses in the IT and business areas. He is also a contributing technical editor to IT Jungle's "The Four Hundred" and "Four Hundred Guru" Newsletters.

A former IBM Senior Systems Engineer, Brian has an active consultancy in the information technology field, (www.kellyconsulting.com). He is the author of many dozens of books and numerous articles about current IT topics. Kelly is a frequent speaker at national conferences, user group meetings across the United States.

This is Brian's fourth book about the injustice and dishonesty brought forth upon Seniors by an unscrupulous and corrupt Congress. Brian would like to see the look on readers' faces after you read this book and you find out how much money would be in your monthly check if Congress had been honest for the last thirty years. Kelly is convinced Seniors can get a lot of that money back in monthly benefits—if we all insist.

This is Brian Kelly's 181st book in various topical areas.

Chapter 1 Hey Buddy, Can you Spare a Dime?

A group of senior citizens march through New York City in 1961, trying to urge the Kennedy administration to add health care coverage to Social Security. Four years later, Social Security was amended to include the transformative programs Medicaid and Medicare.Harry Harris/AP

SSR Benefits raise for 2018 was a net of zero

FYI, there is no official abbreviation for social security or social security retirement. Therefore, in this book we will use our own abbreviation *SSR* to mean social security as well as for social security retirement. As many know, the German Army in World War II commandeered the term SS and, so we will stay away from any negative connotation by staying away from that abbreviation. Think *SSR* for Social Securiy Retirement.

When President Trump was inaugurated in 2017, the paltry increase from President Obama's last year in office was .3%. That is .003 for those like me who want to really know where the decimal point is.

I don't think that President Trump intended to slam Seniors like Obama did; but they got slammed nonetheless . Obama's last approved COLA increment was implemented by the newly elected President Trump. Seniors who think this President does no wrong are now hoping he sees what happened throughout the Obama years and about thirty years before, and that he adjusts things retroactively to where they should be awful close to being right. No senior should have to miss a wholesome meal because their government has cheated them.

The potential benefits increase for millions of Seniors in 2018 was expected to be larger than usual to make up for the past abuses by government in calculating the inflation rate. After Obama's almost-zero last rate at .3%, President Trump's announced rate at 2% was admittedly about six times more than the 4 bucks raise per month in Obama's swan-song.

But it still does not make up for the actual inflation rate's impact on Seniors' income. President Trump must learn this. Moreover, it does nothing to counteract the intentional lowball CPI official inflation rates, endured for over thirty years by Seniors. There was a time thirty years ago when SSR monthly payments were large enough to live. No longer!

Over the years, Government ineptness permitted these payments to lose their value and this cost Seniors many thousands of dollars. Despite this act being fraudulent, the Congress is not naïve. They know exactly what they did.

In government, the left hand takes what the right hand gives. Seniors have already got the bad news early that Medicare premiums for physicians' services rose again in 2017 and with 2018 almost gone, it has happened again. The Medicare Part-B increase consumed the entire cost-of-living adjustment for most Seniors.

The same government that thinks Seniors should get 2% to help with increased costs and out of pocket expenses, is stole back its 2%. Thus none of the higher costs caused by real inflation were mitigated. Seniors lost again. Hey Buddy, Can You Spare A Dime?

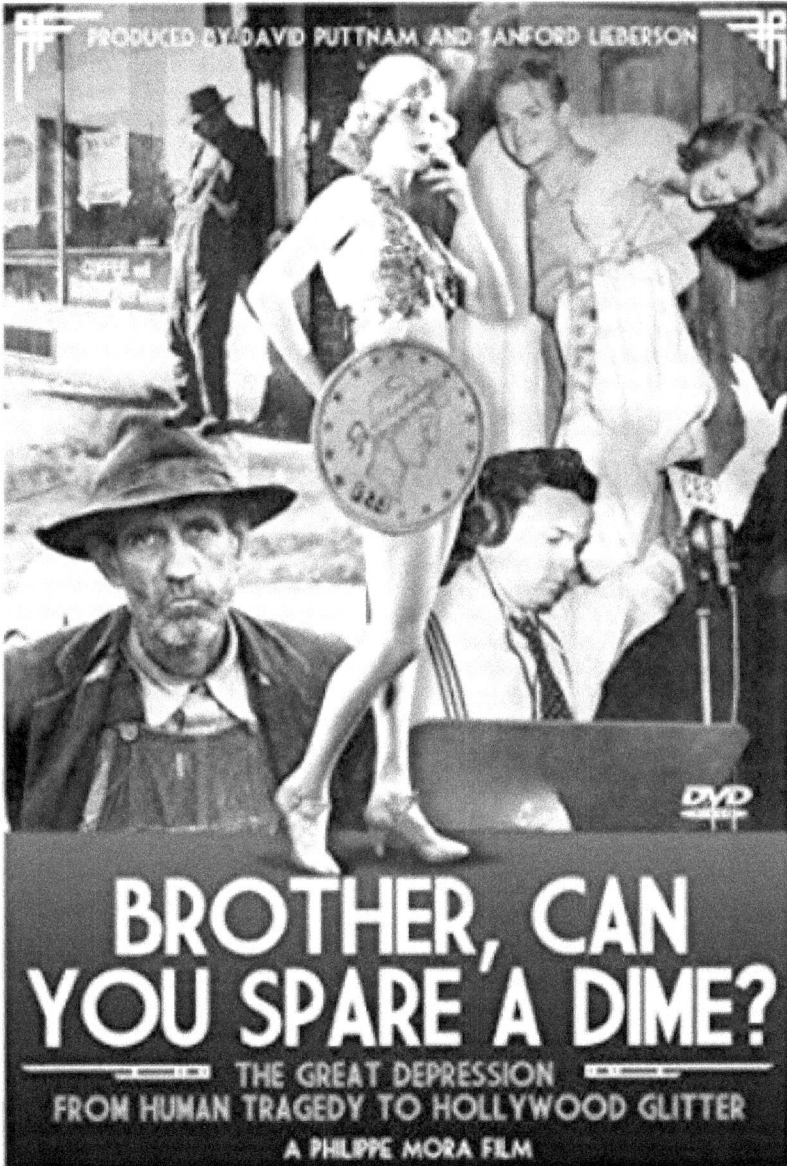

PRODUCED BY DAVID PUTTNAM AND SANFORD LIEBERSON

BROTHER, CAN YOU SPARE A DIME?
THE GREAT DEPRESSION
FROM HUMAN TRAGEDY TO HOLLYWOOD GLITTER
A PHILIPPE MORA FILM

Brother, Can You Spare a Dime? is a 1975 documentary film starring Walt Disney, Bing Crosby, Charlie Chaplin, Andrews Sisters, Fred Astaire, Shirley Temple, Eleanor Roosevelt, and Franklin Delano Roosevelt. It was produced by Image Entertainment, consisting largely of newsreel footage and contemporary film clips to portray the era of the Great Depression and the tough times experienced equally by most Americans.

"Brother, Can You Spare A Dime?"

They used to tell me I was building a dream
And so I followed the mob
When there was earth to plow or guns to bear
I was always there, right on the job

They used to tell me I was building a dream
With peace and glory ahead
Why should I be standing in line
Just waiting for bread?

Once I built a railroad, I made it run
Made it race against time
Once I built a railroad, now it's done
Brother, can you spare a dime?

Once I built a tower up to the sun
Brick and rivet and lime
Once I built a tower, now it's done
Brother, can you spare a dime?

Once in khaki suits, gee, we looked swell
Full of that Yankee Doodly Dum
Half a million boots went slogging through Hell
And I was the kid with the drum

Say, don't you remember? They called me 'Al'
It was 'Al' all the time
Why don't you remember? I'm your pal
Say buddy, can you spare a dime?

Once in khaki suits, ah, gee, we looked swell
Full of that Yankee Doodly Dum
Half a million boots went slogging through Hell
And I was the kid with the drum

Oh, say, don't you remember? They called me 'Al'
It was 'Al' all the time
Say, don't you remember? I'm your pal
Buddy, can you spare a dime?

To the rest of the Country, the Trump era is now bringing in prosperity that has been absent for at least eight years. But, not everybody is gaining. Seniors are still suffering through the Great CPI Depression, with its major inflation tax. So far, there is no recovery in sight for Seniors, but, going into Trump's third year, there is still hope for Seniors.

With what the Congress has done to Seniors, you would swear that every Congressman is either an Ostrich or a buffoon. They have their heads so far into the sand that they can actually say they do not know what they are doing to Seniors. But, they do!

Among other things to cheat Seniors, the legislators know that the healthcare costs for a teenager are lots less than for a senior. Nonetheless, the part of CPI for healthcare is just a bit over 6%. But it costs Seniors 25% of their checks. Try buying a few Lipitor pills on that.

Seniors 65 and older spend more than twice as much on health care, and those 75 and older spend nearly three times more on health care than younger consumers. Congress ignores their plight.

Not only do health care expenditures steadily increase with age but health care costs have also consistently risen much faster than other market basket categories. The current price index known technically as CPI-W, does not take these critical differences in the elderly population into consideration.

Maybe the old white guys in Congress do not need their SSR pensions but they take them anyway. Maybe they have so much money they do not notice but if SSR was all they had, like most Seniors, they'd notice right away. Seniors under this US government for the past 30 years are lucky if they can eat a nutritious meal every day.

I can see no reason why the Congress does not know the perilous predicament in which they place Seniors by their lack of support for senior issues. At election time, other than the Democrats saying Republicans are going to take it all away—all SSR, there is no candidate talking about the fraud, well known to Congress, that keeps Seniors in the poorhouse and then locks the door.

Congress is smart enough to know yet it chooses not to act. They know that Seniors spend a significant portion of their income on out-of-pocket health care expenses not covered by Medicare. As time goes by, each and every year, they also know that more and more of their Social Security benefit checks are eaten up and will continue to be eaten up at a higher rate by rising health care costs.

According to the Medicare Trustees, 33 percent of the average senior's Social Security check will be consumed by Medicare out-of-pocket costs. Today the number is already 25 percent. Yet, the 25 percent is not part of the CPI and so this year's 2% increase did not help pay for increased health care costs.

If it were possible, I would suggest for Seniors to elect their own Congresspersons as there is nobody in Congress, or so it seems who is watching out for our oldest generation—our grandparents and great grandparents. They know but when confronted with facts about the plight of Seniors, they put their heads deeper in the sand.

The truth is that if a candidate for the House or the Senate offered to solve the fraudulent CPI problem for Seniors, they would get almost every senior vote. Any takers out there?

Will Donald Trump come through for Seniors?

It gives me no pleasure to say that Donald Trump has already gotten his two years of good will from Seniors. Will he get another? I say yes because there is no hope from anybody else.

In too many ways, today's times for Seniors remind me of the peasants rotting in the Russian gulags. Looking for any hope, they found every excuse to forgive Joseph Stalin for their plight. "If only Joseph knew!" They believed 100% that somehow if he only knew, Stalin would do something to help them. Yet, Stalin himself was the perpetrator. Congress today is the perpetrator.

Trump has no more than one more year to get it right with Seniors who have been very patient while starving. I would suspect that when the new President finds that fraud was perpetrated by more than thirty years of past administrations on SSR recipients, year after year, he will act. Seniors are counting on it.

Before he acts, he will also find that the average social security monthly benefit today would be way more than double the number that it is. Seniors are asked to live on a figure that should be 450% higher but it has been depleted by the elderly not receiving the correct cost of living raises for well over thirty years. President Donald Trump will find when he finally looks at SSR, that if only the government played by the Roosevelt "deal," Seniors today would not be in such torment.

Try asking a public service union or the unions in my very own city to get by with a 2% raise and then ask if it is OK for you to take it back by charging them a fee or some dues. They would laugh at you as the ravages of inflation are witnessed by the prices in the supermarket. All human beings in America, not just Seniors needed much more than just 2% in 2018 to stay even. Seniors have it worse because the government whacked them the whole 2% for Medicare Part-B.

How about point three percent? We know that unions get three percent or more regardless of the CPI-W inflation rate. If it were 2016, if .3% were a good number, you should have been able to tell your grocer that you would pay no more than .3% of last year's list price even though the grocer asked for 10% more by at the register. These unfortunately are not exaggerations and the Congress knows they are stiffing Seniors every day. Seniors cannot afford to laugh it off.

President Trump, I suspect, is not aware that this fraud has continued through the last 30-years of government and multiple administrations. Like many Seniors, I expect that as soon as he is aware, he will do his best to fix it. I still have faith and I still have hope. Donald Trump is no Joseph Stalin.

The cries of Seniors for help have been ignored for years. And the cheating using a fake CPI is still going on. Congress and the President must be made to fully understand what they have done to the American public.

"In effect, this means that increases in Social Security benefits were minimal, for a third year, for many people, putting them in a bind," said Mary Johnson, Social Security and Medicare policy consultant at the Senior Citizens League in 2016. In a new study, her organization estimates that Seniors have lost one-third of their buying power since 2000 as Social Security cost-of-living adjustments have flattened, and health care and housing costs have soared.

Most of us already see that when we purchase anything, it costs more each time. However, Congress thinks they have gotten away with lying to the public. They have not had to pay at the ballot box for their chicanery as of yet. This book should help solve that problem.

Each year there is hope and then the same government that gives hope, extinguishes it.

Before we turn you over to Chapter Two, which discusses the specifics of the big rip-off that the Congress has perpetrated intentionally upon Seniors, let's go back to the original intention of social security. Many know that President Roosevelt promised Americans who agreed with him, a *retirement with dignity*.

Those who lived through the depression, including my own father, repeated the words *retirement with dignity* whenever they spoke about Roosevelt and his greatest achievement, Social Security. As we know, President Trump likes the term *retirement with dignity*, so we will be looking for positive action from him as his third year unfolds.

•

Chapter 2 The CPI Is a Big Rip-Off for Seniors

Obama hoped to make the CPI even worse for Seniors

For eight years of Obama, Seniors expected nothing from former president Obama and he always delivered exactly as expected—nothing. In fact, on Tuesday October 18, 2016, the stingy Obama Administration released its last percentage increase in benefits for Social Security recipients as almost 65 million senior citizens stood breathless, waiting for the good news.

There was no good news. It was point three percent. In fact, anytime Seniors hold their breath it could be catastrophic. So, the simple fact that there were no known casualties that day, might be the only good news of that day.

Recently as Seniors know, with the many prior zero-level increases and the former president's 2016 most generous .3 percent (point three %) in benefits, Seniors gained no weight around the holidays unless they had the pleasure of visiting somebody else's home not affected by Obama's hand.

How did the fake news occur?

The loving Social Security Administration (SSA) bases the annual cost-of-living adjustment (COLA) on a contrivance known as the consumer price index aka CPI-W. It was and continues to be bogus. The W next to CPI, means that in 1990, the government took even more away from Seniors by under-reporting the actual inflation rate.

This piece of magic formula supposedly tracks the prices of goods and services--including energy, food, and medical care--consumed by urban workers. The government wins when it states lower than actual inflation numbers so the SSA gets to pay less to Seniors from its empty fund. Yes, in America we still call that cheating.

The government simply lies about it and in the October 2016 announcement they admitted it again. Relatively low inflation has meant a small uptick in the index from the last year. Of course, 2015 was the seventh year for Obama. In 2015, his self-guided stingy administration chose zero (COLA) as the former president's favorite number.

Yes, the fake inflation rate released as the gospel two years ago assured that SSR payments did not increase at all from 2015 to 2016. Those of us who have seen the former POTUS do what no other president has done thought perhaps that he was about to rig the first ever decrease in benefits since SSR began. But, I guess he really wanted Hillary to win the presidency and a zero increase would not have helped. If he had actually known there was no down side, who knows?

This year, while a prior version of this book was being written, the first year of President Donald Trump, with a .003 increase financed by former POTUS Obama, additional Seniors entered the poorhouse. Once Seniors enter the poorhouse in recent years, it's like a visit to the Eagles' *Hotel California*:

"Relax," said the night man, "We are programmed to receive You can check out any time you like, but you can never leave!"

Nobody gets out of the poorhouse and nobody gets out of the Hotel California, which might as well be the poorhouse. To escape, President Trump would have to advocate and assure a payback to Seniors of their rightful due. The thirty years of fraud need to be paid back so Seniors can escape both the Hotel California and the poorhouse.

Because they can't afford to make a hot meal, Seniors have the option to enter a mortuary for an eternal visit. Or, perhaps, they can find a life on the streets by the full and always fresh garbage cans of the finest restaurants. You may think I jest but that is how bad it is for many Seniors, especially those fighting local property taxes to not lose their homes.

Of course, there is the chance that with some good stuff from the elite restaurants' garbage cans, they might be able to hold on until their kids find out about how poorly-off their grandparents really are, and they rescue them before past Obama policies kill them. But, whose counting bodies?

Though the four bucks a month is something, as noted, most social security recipients will see their "4 bucks" increase in their benefit disappear due to higher charges for Medicare Part B coverage. If I know this, why doesn't President Trump Know it? Just saying!

Because the mainstream media was 100% in Obama's and then Hillary's camp, few stories told the truth of how the government continued to starve Seniors. Their tactics continued to be fraud and abuse. Perhaps there was some waste there also as they had to spend a lot of money getting the bogus CPI created and disseminated as if it were true. The only benefit of this activity of course is that the Congress is not held accountable for stiffing Seniors. But, now you all know the truth. Blame Congress!

Hard as it may be to believe, there are some good joes out there who like to advocate for older Americans. They think that what the government is doing stinks. They have proof that the inflation measure used to calculate the Social Security COLA doesn't accurately reflect this population's expenses. Seniors have received nothing to help matters because President Obama lied, and he had set up Hillary Clinton so that she could repeat the same lies. We know what happened to her.

How many years of not keeping up with the value of money in terms of purchasing power would it take for you to no longer be able to afford your own city's taxes. How about gasoline? Since Google is run by communists, it is difficult to find the truth when you search for an article to prove a supposition or some words on the street about the plight of Seniors.

It is not just a rumor that steak was originally in the cost-of living market basket but then as the price went up, the price of steak made it clear there was inflation. The SSA took the advice of coffee-breath professors and substituted the price of cheap hamburger meat, and then canned tuna, and then canned cat tuna. It is all true?

Unfortunately, I know that it is true. Good hearted Seniors may not believe that it is true, but it is true, nonetheless. Seniors are hurting and corrupt government officials working with coffee-breath professors made it happen.

Would our wonderful government do that to us just to rig the SSR CPI? If so, I am sure the man who hates rigged things the most, our 45th President, will help solve this properly for Seniors.

Seniors have had years and years of low-ball benefits increases based on lies. These are having a "long-term impact" on retirees, says Mary Johnson, a Social Security policy analyst and researcher for the Senior Citizens League, a nonpartisan lobbying organization. "We have a growing concern."

Despite officials knowing the figures are bogus, social security COLAs are still calculated using CPI-W because placid Seniors fail to complain. Either that or they do not complain loud enough to matter. Seniors have been getting (what's the acceptable word for screwed) for the last thirty or more years.

Obama knew that. It did not matter as long as his objectives were fulfilled. Now, Seniors need to make sure that President Trump, a fair man who likes Seniors, understands that government lies are putting today's Seniors into the poor-house. Why? Because politicians insist that the SSA use fake data to assure that Seniors do not get their proper increments (COLA) that match real inflation.

CPI-W give Seniors an effective pay decrease and that was OK for US administration after administration. Ask Alan Greenspan and ask Newt Gingrich, as much as we all like Newt, if any of this is true. Ask Newt what he did to stop this when he was the big Mahoff in Congress? We will all be astonished and disappointed.

To add reality to the ruse the government regularly puts out, the 2017 cost-of-living raise at .3% did not keep pace with the 5.1% increase in the cost of health care from August 2015 to August 2016, as measured by the Bureau of Labor Statistics.

How is that fair to Seniors? But, who in the Trump Administration is making an issue out of this but me. Yes, I am the only Trumpist doing this. However, despite my attempts anything I say is not official. It should be.

The whole idea that we see is not fair. Every American should know the name of their very own representative. He is part of the Swamp Congress that told government to (what's that respectable word for screw) Seniors in the first place? How can a $100 increase in Medicare not be part of the CPI? Medicare is certainly not the only increase in the cost of living, which Seniors have had to endure each year after their own SSR COLA increase is denied.

With President Trump, Americans are hoping that the oven will be left on long enough to come up with a fully-baked, real solution for the honest needs of the people. Why should Seniors be excluded from the implied fairness clause?

When we consider that the treasury pays as much as $ 500 billion in benefits to illegal aliens, I defy anybody to tell me that if our Congress ran America correctly, we could not afford to make Seniors whole. You bet we can.

Chapter 3 More Proof—System Is Rigged

Some sources calculate cost of living perfectly

Government chooses not to use the true cost of inflation. They know what it is but choose not to use it for the SSR COLA. I just took a run out to a great site that knows that the government is corrupt on the CPI and that its corruption is far-reaching, and it harms Seniors every day.

Shadowstats.com is a web site that has been run by Walter "John" Williams for years. Williams has figured out something that the government does not want you or I to know about.

The Consumer Price Index (CPI) as calculated by the US Bureau of Labor Statistics is manipulated intentionally to produce a lower number than actual so Seniors will be denied their proper benefits increases year after year. These increases, for those that think Seniors are getting raises, are merely brought forth to keep Seniors *even* with inflation. There are no bonuses for Seniors in the formula, When government cheats on the calculations, Seniors lose purchasing power.

The choir should be echoing OOOOH OOOOH—whatever, that sounds like as the government calculated CPI, regardless of its suffix is—a sham.

Government lies all the time and Obama loved to lie about the fake-CPI equating to the cost of living for Seniors because it (what's that name for a respectable term for screwed) them. It never did get it right. It always missed the mark. We all now know that it was intentional.

The government lies were effective v Seniors as they accomplished their mission. They helped the US government; our government save treasury dollars by cheating all Seniors out of their appropriate cost of living increases for years and years and years.

The lie is the most powerful instrument of a corrupt state or as German Minister of Propaganda, Joseph Goebbels said repeatedly: *The truth is the greatest enemy of the state.* Lying about the CPI may not reach that level but permitting this official government lie to continue would be a mistake of similar proportion.

"The truth is the greatest enemy of the state."

Please take the time to examine the chart below (Figure 3-1) so I am able to make my point about the extent of the US government lies with real statistics.

Figure 3-1 Shadow Statistics Reveal the True CPI

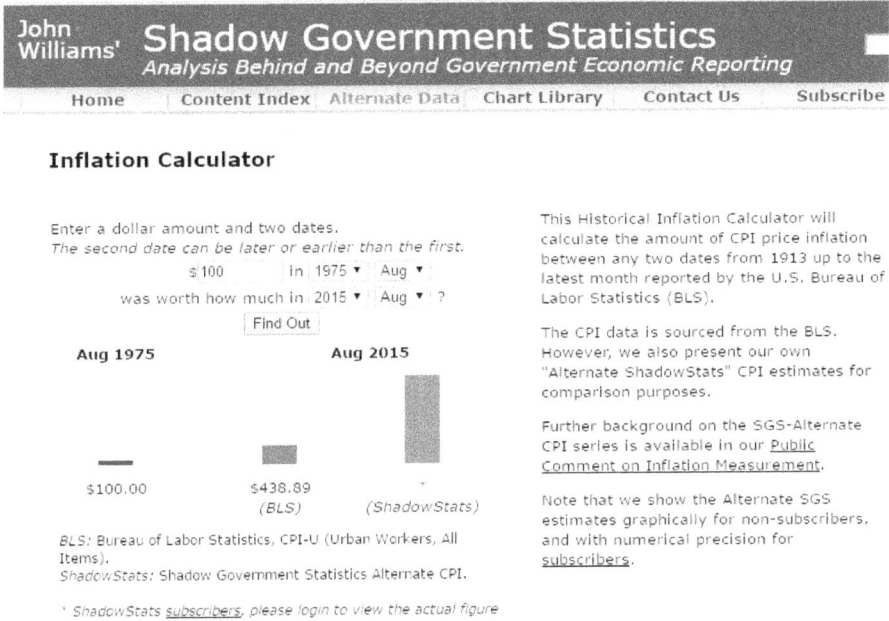

ⓘ www.shadowstats.com/inflation_calculator?amount1=100&y1=1975&m1=8&y2=2015&m2=8&calc=Find+Out

John Williams' Shadow Government Statistics
Analysis Behind and Beyond Government Economic Reporting

Home   Content Index   Alternate Data   Chart Library   Contact Us   Subscribe

Inflation Calculator

Enter a dollar amount and two dates.
The second date can be later or earlier than the first.

$100 in 1975 ▾ Aug ▾
was worth how much in 2015 ▾ Aug ▾ ?

Find Out

Aug 1975   **Aug 2015**

$100.00 $438.89   *
                 (BLS)   (ShadowStats)

BLS: Bureau of Labor Statistics, CPI-U (Urban Workers, All Items).
ShadowStats: Shadow Government Statistics Alternate CPI.

* ShadowStats subscribers, please login to view the actual figure

This Historical Inflation Calculator will calculate the amount of CPI price inflation between any two dates from 1913 up to the latest month reported by the U.S. Bureau of Labor Statistics (BLS).

The CPI data is sourced from the BLS. However, we also present our own "Alternate ShadowStats" CPI estimates for comparison purposes.

Further background on the SGS-Alternate CPI series is available in our Public Comment on Inflation Measurement.

Note that we show the Alternate SGS estimates graphically for non-subscribers, and with numerical precision for subscribers.

Look at the line in the figure where it says *(ShadowStats)* in parenthesis under the vertical green bar. Color can be seen in Kindle but not in hard copy. It is under the words, *Aug 2015* in Figure 3-1.

This 100% accurate information produced by Williams by the way is not provided for free, but it is available and that is very good. Williams' information is available on subscription and should be used by the Trump Administration to correct the lies and make the correct reparation payments to the Seniors who are still alive.

Also on that same "line," you can see when you look real hard that to get this calculator to show the 40-year inflation value from 1975 through 2015, I typed in $100.00 for the value of the money in 1975. The CPI total of $438.89 is the amount that

$100 was worth in August 2015 about forty years later. The value of money never stands still. This is about a 450% difference.

Take the same dime that in 1975 might get you into the local movie theatre and see if they will let you in today. Try to buy a big bag of chips or popcorn for a nickel. Now, you have the idea. The purchasing power of that dime in 1975 was a dime. But the same purchasing power of the dime invested at the true inflation rate is 43.8 cents. In my world this is about 4.38 times the value if 1975. Yet, Seniors are not frolicking in such a 438% increase in benefits. Why not? Government lies... that's why!

I hope that President Trump sees these stats and says to his team: "Brian Kelly is right. Even if I give 15% for each of four or even eight years, Seniors will still be so far behind that we'll have to adjust this properly for some time." My personal hope is that as Seniors begin to die from lack of sustenance, that many who have suffered will not fie and instead will still be around as the President makes this deficit up for Seniors.

In the charts that Williams has on his site, it is plain to see that the numbers do not lie like the government. The government lies. On the average, SSR recipients in the years in which the Obama government gave zero or just about zero, the correct benefit increase based on real inflation should have been 6%. Hopefully President Trump will examine this closely and make the right adjustments for Seniors.

Before we wrap up this chapter, let's peek at the stats of the cost of living (COLA) benefits provided by the eight years Obama administration.

<u>2009-2016 -- 2008 was from Bush</u>

2009	0%
2010	0%
2011	3.6%
2012	1.7%
2013	1.5%
2014	1.7%
2015	0%
2016	.3%

Are those numbers not pathetic? The purchasing power of Seniors hit bottom during Obama's time in office. By the way, the ShadowStats true inflation using the 1980 method for 2011 is 12%. Obama's 3.6% for 2011 was way off the mark and not quite so generous as it may have first seemed. We all lost 12% purchasing power and Mr. Obama gave Seniors back 3.6%. How was that keeping with the Roosevelt deal to keep Seniors whole?

I bet Mr. Barack Obama could not keep Mrs. Barack Obama's incremental budget that low. He would have had to find another bedroom in the White-House for sleeping.

Chapter 4 Will Congress Ever Fix the CPI Problem?

CPI has become a political tool

We have already learned that Walter J. Williams' ShadowStats.com uses the accurate methodology using a standard market basket as a fair and honest approach to determine the real cost of living for Seniors. Nothing is more intolerable in the US today than government's fraudulent taking of earned benefits, in the millions of dollars, from Seniors simply because government has the power to do so.

In an October 2015 campaign speech, Candidate Trump issued a call for wealthy Americans to "voluntarily" give up their Social Security benefits. "I have friends that are worth hundreds of millions and billions of dollars and get Social Security," he said. "They don't even know the check comes in." Trump for president said he could save money for Social Security by "getting rid of fraud."

Trump also notes that Social Security is, as he is known to say, a "deal" between Uncle Sam and American citizens and that the federal government is bound to hold up its end of the bargain. Cheating Seniors for over forty years does not prove the case that government is keeping its side of the bargain.

"It's not unreasonable for people who paid into a system for decades to expect to get their money's worth--that's not an 'entitlement,' that's honoring a deal," he writes in his 2011 book *Time to Get Tough.*

"We as a society must also make an ironclad commitment to providing a safety net for those who can't make one for themselves. Social Security is here to stay. To be sure, we must reform it, root out the fraud, make it more efficient, and ensure that the program is solvent. Same goes for Medicare. Again, people have lived up to their end of the bargain and paid into the program in good faith...Of course they believe they're 'entitled' to receive the benefits they paid—for they are!"

Even financial experts say Trump's call to reform Social Security does have some merit.

"Surprisingly enough, Trump's few comments on Social Security could actually be the start of an effective overhaul," says Chris Carosa, a retirement specialist and author of the book, Hey! What's My Number? How to Improve the Odds You Will Retire in Comfort."

It all starts with not cutting benefits to those within 15 to 20 years of retirement -- i.e. those 50 and over -- something only Trump is adamant about."

Social Security prevents approximately 26 million Seniors from falling below the poverty line each year. When anybody, especially a senior on just SSR, is on a fixed income – that right now is a mere $14,000 per year on average, there is no provision to deal with the ever-increasing costs of healthcare, prescriptions, and housing. And so, this creates a situation that breaks the promises made 80 years ago when social security began.

Chapter 5 How to Pay for the Senior SSR Boost?

Getty Images

Can the US afford to pay for Seniors to be OK?

I say that we cannot afford not to do what is right. This is America! If we can afford to give the biggest banks a $16 trillion bailout we can afford to fix social security and give Seniors a make-up payment to keep them out of the poorhouse. There are lots of other ways to pay for it but first the government must accept that they (what's that proper word that can be use din place of screwed) Seniors for years.

If somebody says we cannot afford to assure that Seniors can lead lives in which the poorhouse is not a constant threat, please tell them to remember the promise of Franklin D. Roosevelt about Constant dollars for those collecting. Not one dollar should be paid in welfare to illegal aliens if we deny Seniors of their rightful benefits.

I have confidence that OMB Director Mick Mulvaney is as sharp as a tack. He is so good with numbers he can look everywhere to find a way to make Seniors whole and like Trump says, make the benefits means tested so that billionaires do not collect. We can afford making senior citizens on SSR whole again; and we must. We're smart enough to get the job done.

Today's Social Security dilemma began after Lyndon Johnson permitted the SSR Trust Fund to be robbed to pay for his social welfare programs in the late 1960's.

Then sometime in the 1980's the dirtiest politicians in America colluded with coffee-breath professors in Academia so they would not have to take the real cost of living into consideration when calculating the percentage increase in senior's benefits, AKA COLA.

They contrived notions such as CPI-U, CPI-W, and the Chained CPI—all schemes to reduce COLA and return dollars to the treasury from the backs of senior citizens.

All SSR recipients wanted was what Roosevelt promised. They wanted to be paid in constant dollars. None of the CPI calculations do that.

None of these machinations were intended to provide the true cost of living and/or the true out of pocket expense increases endured by senior citizens who were fortunate enough to that point to be able to survive in America.

Nobody in America wants this perpetration to stand, especially Seniors who are about to lose their homes and who are scraping to find their next substantial meal.

There are lots of small US budget items that can be eliminated or reduced substantially. These can pay for a proper COLA with make-up provisions for Seniors. Among these are the Department of Energy, The EPA, and the

Department of Education. There are lots others. We need none of these agencies that are duplicates of state agencies

I am sure the Trump team and the few members of Congress who represent the people can handle the deep thinking. The secret is to find some really big items out there.

Two of biggest items to help are the annual cost savings from solving the problem of 60 million illegal residents in the US. On the low-side, this can save us about $180 Billion a year. On the high side, it exceeds $500 Billion per year. Nobody from another country should receive welfare or SSR when Americans are shut out.

The next major item is a one-time revenue opportunity or a continual flow depending on how we do it. It is huge. It will come from imposing a 10% tax on all oil extracted from the US. This will provide $1,531,200,000,000 in total over the years. That's trillion with a T. That should keep us going for many years.

Maybe it would be OK if Seniors were paid back more than needed but I am not suggesting that. The fact is the make-up COLAS at 15% for eight years can certainly be paid even if these "how-to" estimates are way off.

Donald Trump once said that he could pay off the national debt with the oil reserves that are in this country. Using new estimates that prove that the US has more reserves than any other country—at least 264 billion barrels, we are sitting on a lot of black gold with much of it on public lands.

From verified calculations, it is now fact that Seniors on SSR are owed about $4.5 dollars for every dollar in benefits received in their monthly e-checks. Seniors therefore receive

$3.50 less than due against each dollar they receive because of the inherent fraud in the new versions of the CPI.

Seniors are not greedy and therefore do not need to be paid back all at once. A 15% per year COLA for eight years—even just four years—would go a long way in getting Seniors back on track. In my opinion, and by now it is surely your opinion also, this is a debt due from theft by government. It is not a gift.

The cost of providing social security benefits is huge at about $900 billion per year. Providing a 15% make-up COLA for Seniors beginning in 2019, and continuing for four years to start can be handled by a combination of cost savings and revenue from oil and the great mind of Mick Mulvaney. .

The oil reserve is a major bonanza. Together, the savings in immigration costs, and the revenue from the 10% tax on oil extraction can keep social security going forever if our politicians have the political will to do the right thing.

Can you imagine the savings when we discover that 60 million, not 11 million illegal aliens live in America?

Chapter 6 Solution Review: Pay Back the Senior Rip-Off

Mike Huckabee is for Seniors

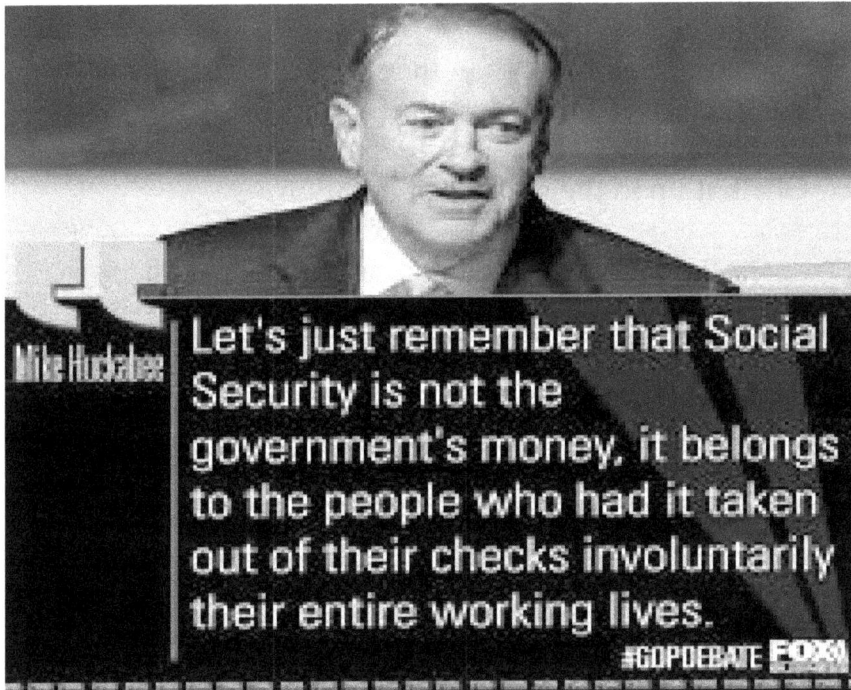

Let's just remember that Social Security is not the government's money, it belongs to the people who had it taken out of their checks involuntarily their entire working lives.

#GOPDEBATE FOX

Mike Huckabee was the first brave Republican to complain when he publicly accused "illegals, prostitutes, pimps, (and) drug dealers" of freeloading off the Social Security system during the first GOP primary debate way back on August. 6, 2015.

The government will not admit nor publish the costs registered in the SSR system that are caused by generous government workers out in the field certifying illegals as eligible.

Mike Huckabee knows the truth as do many other politicos, who, unlike Huckabee, choose to do nothing to help America. This freeloading has been free to everybody but the Seniors who paid the toll for years. I am counting on President Trump to repay Seniors for all the past pilferage.

During his campaign, candidate Trump promised to protect Social Security without cutting benefits. I wrote this book to help remind Seniors as well as our 45th President that protecting SSR is a great notion that must be done with sharp teeth.

However, Seniors need more than the status quo that put them behind what's fair over for the last thirty years or so. Seniors should be receiving $4.50 for every 1975 dollar received today. It is a fact. Chalk it up to the ravages of inflation.

Senior citizens have been cheated and need to be paid back for the abuses to the system over the years. Mike Huckabee and other brave Americans have cited these. It is an obligation of America.

The obligation includes paying back Medicare from Obamacare and by increasing SSR benefits over the next eight years (at least four years) of the two Trump terms by at least 15% per year. The second four years of 15% would end the cries to make Seniors whole, though it would only be half or so of what is owed.

It would be wonderful if President Trump gets eight years in total and he keeps the flow of benefit increases so that when he departs, it is at least the same as the true cost of living (Average of 6% higher than the CPI).

Review: Boost Social Security Now!

In this review, we will go over the whole issue using a summary format at times and we will introduce a few more notions while summarizing.

Social Security has become a taboo issue to discuss in political campaigns anymore because, since the Obama years, Democrats no longer have a love affair with Seniors. It is no longer publicly discussed by our duplicitous media despite the fact that Seniors' issues need the spotlight now more than ever as we have discussed. Of course every Democratic candidate is using their time-tested liars playbook, which includes scare tactics to intimidate Seniors about losing everything if Republicans are elected. Shame on the Democrats for sure.

This is the same Democratic Party that was throwing Granny off the cliff just a few years ago. Now, they simply point at their candidate's opponent and they say that he wants to lower Social Security. Only a fool would want to do that, but Democrats know that play has worked in every election because Democrats deep down want to believe the lie. I am a Democrat but over the last few years I could not keep up with their lies, so I know that I cannot believe them.

The Democrat-controlled media projects an image of Seniors that they are greedy. They all in unison derided the implied greed of SSR recipients who received a whopping two percent cost of living raise to kick off 2018. Democrats are obviously oblivious to the fact that the true inflation rate for 2017 was nearly 11%. It was not 2%, but 11%.

No wonder Seniors are struggling when their cost for purchases goes up 11% and their COLA to make up for that is a mere 2%. These are 2017 cost of living figures. How do I know that, and most don't? It is not popular for Democrats to tell the truth or to provide any facts when they implicate the Party in this travesty.

By the way, if Obama had his way with the chained CPI, a contrivance he supported against his advisor's wishes, as bad as it is, it would be even worse for Seniors today. Seniors all know that the former president gave zero cost increases three times during his presidency showing all Democrats lack-of-love for Seniors.

"It's squeezing them. It's causing them to dip into savings more quickly," said Mary Johnson of The Senior Citizens League. "The lifetime income that they were counting on just isn't there."

In 2014, President Obama pushed hard for advancing a surreptitious reduction of Social Security benefits by using the fraudulent chained-CPI mechanism. Obama's dubious market calculations would have cost retirees more than 2 percent of their incomes. Chained-CPI is a Democrat innovation in concert with liberal economists and coffee-breath professors. Yet, today all Democrats are blaming the chained CPI on Republicans. That of course is a lie but try to get a Democrat to believe that it is not true.

There are several ways senior Americans can investigate how much government lies cost them each year. The government purposely underestimates the cost of living using CPI-W or chained CPI to deprive the elderly of a commensurate actual increase in earned benefits. One such method for you to use to calculate your personal loss to government fraud each year is to subscribe to the Chapwood index or as discussed in previous chapters, you may explore Shadowstats.com. In these sources there is proof-a-plenty, and the information is not government propaganda.

Seniors unfortunately are running out of whatever financial cushions they may ever have had, and their plight today is dire. I encourage you all to research the degree to which government deceptions are resulting in these surreptitious deprivations.

After decades of Americans being saturated by our mainstream propaganda rags, it is refreshing to finally see the truth in print. The Chapwood Index reflects the true cost-of-living increase in America. It is updated and released twice a year. There, the ruses or mis-directions of the government are not included in its pages. The fraudulent government CPI is debunked on its site.

Instead, it truthfully reports the unadjusted actual cost and price fluctuation of the top 500 items on which Americans spend their after-tax dollars in the 50 largest cities in the nation. It is as Franklin D. Roosevelt intended it to be.

It exposes why middle-class Americans—salaried workers who are given routine pay hikes and retirees who depend on annual increases in their corporate pension and Social Security payments—cannot maintain their standard of living. Plainly and simply, the Index shows that their income cannot keep up with their expenses and it explains why they increasingly have to turn to the government for supplementation.

Mainstream Democrats such as Nancy Pelosi, Maxine Waters, and Chuck Schumer exacerbate the situation by allowing the use of even more inequitable methods such as the new chained CPI to help assure that Seniors can languish in poverty as soon as possible.

The problem of lacking transparency on true costs (true inflation) occurs because salary and benefit increases are pegged to the fraudulent Consumer Price Index (CPI), which for more than a century has purported to reflect the fluctuation in prices for a typical "basket of goods" in American cities — but which actually hasn't done that for the last 30 to 40 years.

The middle class has seen its purchasing power decline dramatically in the last three decades, forcing more and more people to seek welfare help from the government when their savings are gone. And as long as pay raises and benefit increases are tied to a false CPI, this trend will continue.

How many of your friends have said "how can they say there is no inflation when we see it in our insurance premiums, at the gas pump, and in the supermarket?". Are we to believe that our government lives on a different planet? Democrats believe that Seniors will not question their lies and so they keep buying the wool to pull over the eyes of US Seniors.

In the past, nobody was anxious to throw the proverbial grandma under the bus. Now, believe it or not, hordes of constituencies are lining up to be the first to fleece what should belong to her, into the eternal abyss, never to be seen again. The list of offenders includes: Congress, government officials, professors in academia, the "greatest" economic advisors the world has ever known, and dejected stand-alone economists who failed to gain tenure at any university.

This group of elite misfits have formed a diabolical consortium to cheat Seniors out of their due cost of living increases promised from the very day the SSR act was passed in 1935 by Franklin Delano Roosevelt.

As the mainstream Democrats kowtow to cultural elites and financial institutions, turning their backs on the workers and middle-class that defined their constituency for much of the 20th century, it is up to us, regular Americans, to pick up the slack and fight for the rights of all everyday Americans.

There are many good candidates running against Democrats who have vowed to keep Seniors down. One such candidate is Lou Barletta, running against Bob Casey Jr. in Pennsylvania for the US Senate. Another is John Chrin, who is another mainstay on the pro-senior team. If Congress could be dumped and replaced, it would be people like Barletta and Chrin who would be effective replacements to assure Seniors got back on their feet.

When SSR was enacted, the president promised full dollar value throughout the years in order to ensure its passage in 1935. We cannot let this be undermined by the likes of Chuck Schumer and Nancy Pelosi.

Many Americans are concerned that the Social Security program itself may not be able to sustain itself while others see the government cheating on the cost of living increases (CPI) thereby predetermining a life of squalor for Seniors.

All successful societies throughout the ages, have maintained respect and dignity for their elders. Not only is cheating Seniors a moral failure, it is a sign of a civilization entering an era of decay.

While Seniors are losing their homes and many, for want of bread and milk, are on the verge of heading to the proverbial poorhouse or worse—the clutches of the Grim Reaper, Congress in 2018 pretended to care, giving a 2% raise, but then quickly snatched it right back in the dead of night via a Medicare Part B premium increase. This additional Medicare Part B charge for necessary health services for Seniors was excluded from the cost of living calculations. How could Congress have missed that?

Thus, to pay Medicare part B, Seniors have been forced to use their "generous" 2% raise, rather than to offset the costs brought forth from inflation in 2017 for which the 2% was intended. Since the real inflationary cost increases were closer to 11% according to the index, that means that instead of 9% that Seniors were to endure, they actually accrued a full load of 11% in price increases. It's easy to understand why this constant drainage of resources is unsustainable for senior citizens. More and more are forced to go to welfare or give up as their homes are foreclosed.

How did we reach this point?

This is a more complete review of why that which the Bureau of Labor Statistics (BLS) calls the consumer price index (CPI). The CPI has been a bogus number for so long, Americans have often concluded that the government is cheating in the calculation.

Early in the administration of disgraced former President Bill Clinton, an economist named Michael Boskin, and Alan Greenspan, Chairman of the Board of Governors of the Federal Reserve System, devised a scheme that would allow for market basket "substitutions" to artificially lower the cost of living and result in lower treasury payments to our oldest Americans.

These guys found value in having senior citizens help save the big government money. Prior to their involvement, the consumer price index (CPI) was measured using the cost of a fixed basket of goods, a fairly simple and straightforward concept.

The identical basket of goods would be priced at prevailing market costs for each period, and the period-to-period change in the cost of that market basket represented the rate of inflation in terms of maintaining a constant standard of living. That was self-evidently fair and reasonable, and predictably resulted in Seniors receiving annual COLA increases in tandem with the prices of goods actually increasing.

But Boskin and Alan Greenspan argued that when one item in the basket, for instance, *steak*, became too expensive, the consumer would substitute hamburger for the steak, and that the inflation measure should reflect the costs tied to buying hamburger rather than the steak. Eventually, it became OK for the bureaucrats to replace the cost of hamburger in the basket with less expensive tuna and eventually because the protein value was the same, cat tuna replaced regular tuna in the market basket.

The Bureaucrats like to tell observers that Seniors did not have to eat the cat tuna, but their basket costs would be the same if they did since the protein value was identical.

In simple terms, the government began to play games with Seniors via the SSR annual inflation adjustments (COLA). It was intentional. To further obscure the true cost of living, other items were selectively removed from the basket when the prices were high and then reinserted when the prices were low. The objective was to save the government money, not to make sure that things were fair for elderly Americans.

Many people have been familiar with this ruse. For example, an economic commentator named Barry Ritholtz joked that Greenspan's core inflation metric can more accurately be described as "inflation ex-inflation," meaning inflation after all of the inflation has been excluded. This demonstrates that the deception of Seniors by the US government has been intentional, and it continues with a new notion called the chained CPI. This complicated measurement will cost Seniors even more. We need all House members and Senators, and President Trump to get this back on track.

The fact is that government has deceitfully stolen directly from the pockets of our beloved Seniors by denying them a fair cost of living increase just to stay even. Some have even suggested that the government believes a natural limit on complaints exists so they won't get caught in their own ruse. They think they will get no criticism because over time, many of the complainants will be silenced by their deaths when they can no longer afford to pay up. Charming thought?

Walter J. Williams, an American blessing who operates the Shadowstats site has demonstrated that Seniors have been stiffed by much more than just 125% and in fact should be receiving more than 4 times what their dollars were worth in 1975. That's $450 instead of $100.00.

Any senior would love to have even a small proportion of that loss back. Government lies cost $350.00 since 1975. But nobody will ever see that and even great representatives, are not telling Americans back home that it is happening.

I hope I have convinced you all that Seniors have been ripped off and are being ripped off financially all the time by their own government. Congress is the real culprit.

So, what do I recommend for now? First of all, you're your Congressperson home for good but tell them why before you do. A current representative has voted for years in favor of those who stiffed Seniors to the point of their giving up. Also, send as many RINOS and Democrats home as you can. Both of these anti-American, anti-Senior representatives ought to be begging for our forgiveness. They won't so let's send in the well-qualified replacement players—whoever is running against them.

Yes, please, in their stead, please vote for the other guy.

A gradual remedy for Seniors, since it would be difficult to give Seniors the proper increase immediately needed to offset this total quagmire caused by government malfeasance, my recommendation would be to approach it gradually, in a way that Seniors would be somewhat pleased, and be able to live out their golden years in a much more dignified manner. Who can argue with that?

For the next four years, and perhaps the four after that, the COLA boost that I'd recommend would be 15% above the real inflation rate as calculated by the index. After four consecutive years, that should be sufficient to remove Seniors from the on-deck circle they currently occupy directly outside the homeless shelter.

That's all it would take. Then we can use the measurements that were in effect before the government fraud, in which a dollar was a dollar and a dime was a dime, and the US must vow to never stiff Seniors again.

Thank you, dear readers, for your attention on these important matters.

In conclusion, I must again express my gratitude for your consideration and any support as we work together to make America even greater. God bless America and help us all make her better!

Other Books by Brian Kelly: (amazon.com, and Kindle)

Millennials Say America Was "Never That Great": Too many pleased days of political chumps not over!
White People Are Bad! Bad! Bad! In 2018, too many people find race as a non-equalizer.
It's Time for The John Doe Party... Don't you think? By By Elephants.
Great Players in Florida Gators Football... Tim Tebow and a ton of other great players
Great Coaches in Florida Gators Football... The best coaches in Gator history.
The Constitution by Hamilton, Jefferson, Madison, et al. The Real Constitution
The Constitution Companion. Will help you learn and understand the Constitution
Great Coaches in Clemson Football The best Clemson Coaches right to Dabo Swinney
Great Players in Clemson Football The best Clemson players in history
Winning Back America. America's been stolen and can be won back completely
The Founding of America... Great book to pick up a lot of great facts
Defeating America's Career Politicians. The scoundrels need to go.
Midnight Mass by Jack Lammers... You remember what it was like Great story
The Bike by Jack Lammers... Great heartwarming Story by Jack
Wipe Out All Student Loan Debt--Now! Watch the economy go boom!
No Free Lunch Pay Back Welfare! Why not pay it back?
Deport All Millennials Now!!! Why they deserve to be deported and/or saved
DELETE the EPA, Please! The worst decisions to hurt America
Taxation Without Representation 4th Edition Should we throw the TEA overboard again?
Four Great Political Essays by Thomas Dawson
Top Ten Political Books for 2018... Cliffnotes Version of 10 Political Books
Top Six Patriotic Books for 2018... Cliffnotes version of 6 Patriotic Boosk
Why Trump Got Elected!.. It's great to hear about a great milestone in America!
The Day the Free Press Died. Corrupt Press Lives on!
Solved (Immigration) The best solutions for 2018
Solved II (Obamacare, Social Security, Student Debt) Check it out; They're solved.
Great Moments in Pittsburgh Steelers Football... Six Super Bowls and more.
Great Players in Pittsburgh Steelers Football ,,,Chuck Noll, Bill Cowher, Mike Tomin, etc.
Great Coaches in New England Patriots Football,,, Bill Belichick the one and only plus others
Great Players in New England Patriots Football... Tom Brady, Drew Bledsoe et al.
Great Coaches in Philadelphia Eagles Football..Andy Reid, Doug Pederson & Lots more
Great Players in Philadelphia Eagles Football Great players such as Sonny Jurgenson
Great Coaches in Syracuse Football All the greats including Ben Schwartzwalder
Great Players in Syracuse Football. Highlights best players such as Jim Brown & Donovan McNabb
Millennials are People Too !!! Give US millennials help to live American Dream
Brian Kelly for the United States Senate from PA: Fresh Face for US Senate
The Candidate's Bible. Don't pray for your campaign without this bible
Rush Limbaugh's Platform for Americans... Rush will love it
Sean Hannity's Platform for Americans... Sean will love it
Donald Trump's New Platform for Americans. Make Trump unbeatable in 2020
Tariffs Are Good for America! One of the best tools a president can have
Great Coaches in Pittsburgh Steelers Football Sixteen of the best coaches ever to coach in pro football.
Great Moments in New England Patriots Football Great football moments from Boston to New England
Great Moments in Philadelphia Eagles Football. The best from the Eagles from the beginning of football.
Great Moments in Syracuse Football The great moments, coaches & players in Syracuse Football
Boost Social Security Now! Hey Buddy Can You Spare a Dime?
The Birth of American Football. From the first college game in 1869 to the last Super Bowl
Obamacare: A One-Line Repeal Congress must get this done.
A Wilkes-Barre Christmas Story A wonderful town makes Christmas all the better
A Boy, A Bike, A Train, and a Christmas Miracle A Christmas story that will melt your heart
Pay-to-Go America-First Immigration Fix
Legalizing Illegal Aliens Via Resident Visas Americans-first plan saves $Trillions. Learn how!
60 Million Illegal Aliens in America!!! A simple, America-first solution.
The Bill of Rights By Founder James Madison Refresh your knowledge of the specific rights for all
Great Players in Army Football Great Army Football played by great players..
Great Coaches in Army Football Army's coaches are all great.
Great Moments in Army Football Army Football at its best.
Great Moments in Florida Gators Football Gators Football from the start. This is the book.
Great Moments in Clemson Football CU Football at its best. This is the book.

Great Moments in Florida Gators Football Gators Football from the start. This is the book.
The Constitution Companion. A Guide to Reading and Comprehending the Constitution
The Constitution by Hamilton, Jefferson, & Madison – Big type and in English
PATERNO: The Dark Days After Win # 409. Sky began to fall within days of win # 409.
JoePa 409 Victories: Say No More! Winningest Division I-A football coach ever
American College Football: The Beginning From before day one football was played.
Great Coaches in Alabama Football Challenging the coaches of every other program!
Great Coaches in Penn State Football the Best Coaches in PSU's football program
Great Players in Penn State Football The best players in PSU's football program
Great Players in Notre Dame Football The best players in ND's football program
Great Coaches in Notre Dame Football The best coaches in any football program
Great Players in Alabama Football from Quarterbacks to offensive Linemen Greats!
Great Moments in Alabama Football AU Football from the start. This is the book.
Great Moments in Penn State Football PSU Football, start--games, coaches, players,
Great Moments in Notre Dame Football ND Football, start, games, coaches, players
Cross Country with the Parents A great trip from East Coast to West with the kids
Seniors, Social Security & the Minimum Wage. Things Seniors need to know.
How to Write Your First Book and Publish It with CreateSpace
The US Immigration Fix--It's all in here. Finally, an answer.
I had a Dream IBM Could be #1 Again The title is self-explanatory
WineDiets.Com Presents The Wine Diet Learn how to lose weight while having fun.
Wilkes-Barre, PA; Return to Glory Wilkes-Barre City's return to glory
Geoffrey Parsons' Epoch... The Land of Fair Play Better than the original.
The Bill of Rights 4 Dummmies! This is the best book to learn about your rights.
Sol Bloom's Epoch ...Story of the Constitution The best book to learn the Constitution
America 4 Dummmies! All Americans should read to learn about this great country.
The Electoral College 4 Dummmies! How does it really work?
The All-Everything Machine Story about IBM's finest computer server.
ThankYou IBM! This book explains how IBM was beaten in the computer marketplace by neophytes

Amazon.com/author/brianwkelly
Brian W. Kelly has written 181 books. Thank you for buying this one.

www.ingramcontent.com/pod-product-compliance
Lightning Source LLC
Chambersburg PA
CBHW072021290326
41934CB00009BA/2153